YOUR KNOWLEDGE H

- We will publish your bachelor's and master's thesis, essays and papers

- Your own eBook and book - sold worldwide in all relevant shops

- Earn money with each sale

Upload your text at www.GRIN.com and publish for free

Imprint:

Copyright © 2017 GRIN Verlag, Open Publishing GmbH
Print and binding: Books on Demand GmbH, Norderstedt Germany
ISBN: 9783668600188

This book at GRIN:

https://www.grin.com/document/385917

Frederick Omoyoma Odorige

Introduction to the Approaches of Just Wars and Bad Peace

Nigerian Peace Keeping and Conflict Resolution since 1960

GRIN Publishing

GRIN - Your knowledge has value

Since its foundation in 1998, GRIN has specialized in publishing academic texts by students, college teachers and other academics as e-book and printed book. The website www.grin.com is an ideal platform for presenting term papers, final papers, scientific essays, dissertations and specialist books.

Visit us on the internet:

http://www.grin.com/

http://www.facebook.com/grincom

http://www.twitter.com/grin_com

Introduction to the approaches of Just Wars and Bad Peace: Nigerian Peace Keeping and Conflict Resolution since 1960

Frederick Omoyoma Odorige

National University of Public Service Hungary

December 2017

I hope it will be lasting, and that Mankind will at length, as they call themselves reasonable Creatures, have Reason and Sense enough to settle their Differences without cutting Throats; for, in my opinion, there was never a good War, or a bad Peace.[1]

Benjamin Franklin. July 27, 1783

Content

---

[1] King, B. (2005, April 22). *Daily Reckoning,* Benjamin Franklin, Diplomat: There Never Was a Good War or a Bad Peace: Ben Franklin. https://dailyreckoning.com/benjamin-franklin-diplomat-there-never-was-a-good-war-or-a-bad-peace-ben-franklin/ Rerieved 11 November 2017

Abstract

The current global security consciousness, terrorist acts and threats have been worsened by unending national and regional conflicts. We are at a crossroad to ascertain the justifications of these conflicts and the role that countries play either to restore peace or to exacerbate the crises.

The main aim of this paper is to introduce the activities of Nigeria at peacekeeping, peace building and peace enforcement across and within her national borders. The research is intended to be assessed on the background of global norms. The result of the review is to examine the gaps and challenges in order to proffer subsequent recommendations for improvement.

This research has become necessary for two reasons. Firstly, the seemingly unending conflicts has led to continuing insecurity, fear, suspicion, wanton destruction of lives, properties and refugee outflow. Therefore, this research is set to pursue the basic goal of the United Nations which is 'to promote international cooperation and to achieve peace and security.'

Secondly, Nigeria as a subject matter, is in tandem with her enviable position and role in peacekeeping since 1960. Furthermore, apart from the fact that Nigeria is respected among the comity of nations; she is one of the largest African countries in terms of population and natural resources, commanding a huge economic value chain within and outside Africa.

Introduction

One of the very active contributors to peace making and peacekeeping in Africa and the United Nations is the Federal Republic of Nigeria. She began her first Peacekeeping effort in 1960 in the Congo- just the same year that she gained independence from colonial Britain. With an estimated population of 180 million people, it is country rich in multi-ethnicity, situated in West Africa. It is surrounded by Niger in the north, the Atlantic Ocean in the south, Cameroon and Chad in the east and Benin in the west.

Nigerian peacekeeping operates under the regional body of the Economic Community of West African States Monitoring Group, (ECOMOG) the African Union (AU) and the larger all-encompassing body of the United Nations.

The forerunner of the United Nations was the League of Nations, an organization conceived in similar circumstances during the first World War, and established in 1919 under the Treaty of Versailles *"to promote international cooperation and to achieve peace and security."*[2]

Peacekeeping is third party intervention in an area of conflict in order to return conflict to peace. This is achieved through the three basic principles of 1. Consent of the parties 2. Impartiality 3. Non-use of force except in self-defence and defence of the mandate[3]

Depending on the mandate received from the Security Council, the process of peacekeeping could also apply Robust peacekeeping which „involves the use of force at the tactical level with the authorization of the Security Council and consent of the host nation and/or the main parties to the conflict.

By contrast, peace enforcement does not require the consent of the main parties and may involve the use of military force at the strategic or international level, which is normally prohibited for Member States under Article 2 (4) of the Charter, unless authorized by the Security Council.[4]

The UN charter is the foundation document of the body. Its laws which empower the UN Security Council to embark on peacekeeping rests on Chapter VI ... "Pacific Settlement of Disputes".

Chapter VII contains provisions related to "Action with Respect to the Peace, Breaches of the Peace and Acts of Aggression'.

Chapter VIII of the Charter provides for the involvement of regional arrangements and agencies in the maintenance of international peace and security provided such activities are consistent with the purposes and principles outlined in Chapter I of the Charter.[5]

---

[2] United Nations. http://www.un.org/en/history-united-nations/index.html Rerieved 11 November 2017
[3] United Nations Peacekeeping. Principles of peacekeeping http://peacekeeping.un.org/en/principles-of-peacekeeping Retrieved 10 November 2017
[4] ibid.
[5] United Nations Peacekeeping. Mandate and the legal basis for peacekeeping http://peacekeeping.un.org/en/mandates-and-legal-basis-peacekeeping. Retrieved 10 November 2017

As an evidence of her interest in peacekeeping, a special training center for Nigerian peacekeepers was established in 2004 at the Peacekeeping Wing (PKW) of the Nigerian Army Infantry Corps Centre. In 2009 it was *upgraded and made an autonomous training institution in 2009 with a new name: the Nigerian Army Peacekeeping Centre (NAPKC). The center undertakes research and delivers training that contributes to peace support operations worldwide. NAPKC was established primarily to give Nigerian troops pre-deployment training on Peace Support Operations. To date, NAPKC has delivered over 230 courses and trained over 53,000 peacekeepers*[6]

In furtherance to this, the Peacekeeping office of the Nigeria Police was established in 2005 with a vision to *„research, train and deploy for global peace support operation*[7] and a mission *„to equip personnel with requisite skills and competencies required to meet complex peace support operations environment through the delivery of quality internationally recognized and professional training."*[8]

Nigeria's desire to embark in Peacekeeping is hinged on her belief and avowed concern on security issues within and outside the country because she believes that her internal security is connected with regional and global security. This fact is guided by the Constititution of the country as entrenched in Chapter 2 section 14. 2 (b) *The security and welfare of the people shall be the primary purpose of government.*

The role played by Nigeria in resolving various conflicts in other Africa countries resonates across her national boundaries especially her role in the wars and conflicts of Congo 1960-1964, Namibia, Angola, Western Sahara, Cambodia, Mozambique, Somalia, Rwanda, Yugoslavia, Bosnia-Herzegovina, Croatia, Macedonia, East Timor, Kosovo, Sierra-Leonean war of 1991-2002, Liberian wars of 1989 – 1996; 1999-2003, Afghanistan, Cote D'Ivoire, Burundi, Haiti, Sudan, South Sudan and Guinea Bissau and the power tussle of Gambia in 2017. Nigeria has participated in over 40 UN peacekeeping operations.

Ironically, Nigeria has been faced with various internal ethnic and religious crises since 1960. Since the coup of 1966, there was the civil war of 1967, the Maitatsine crises of the 1980s, the intermittent Christian-Muslim clashes, the Mohammed coup of 1975, the Dimka coup of 1976 the Buhari coup of 1983, the Babangida coup of 1985 the crises that emanated from the annulment of the 1993 election, and the Abacha coup of 1994; other religious clashes in Aba 2000, Kano 2001 and Kaduna in 2002 among others. These were heightened by the militancy in the Niger Delta since the 1990s and the Boko haram menace in the north east of the country since 26 July 2009.

Most of the conflicts that have led to wars were mostly caused by the silence of the international community in respect of the supposed 1sovereignty' of countries. Such procrastinations have led to the loss of lives especially against innocent people who were not the root cause of the conflicts.

---

[6] Adeniyi. A, Peacekeeping Contributor Profile: Nigeria,
http://www.providingforpeacekeeping.org/2015/04/24/peacekeeping-contributor-profile-nigeria Retrieved 10 November 2017
[7] Nigeria Police Force, http://www.npf.gov.ng/peace_keeping.php Retrieved 10 November 2017
[8] ibid.

A characteristic of some wars is that some global wars have been fought by proxy through financial, military and personnel supports. For example, an overall conclusion was reached that *the United States most likely has been responsible since WWII for the deaths of between 20 and 30 million people in wars and conflicts scattered over the world.*[9]

What is war? War has simply been defined by the English Oxford Living dictionary as *a state of armed conflict between different countries or different groups within a country*.[10] For the sake of this research, the expanded definition of war shall rest on the definitions preferred by the Human Security Report Project as quoted by Our World in Data[11] which is as follows:

- A conflict is coded as a war when the battle-death toll reaches 1,000 or more in a given calendar year.
- An extrastate armed conflict is a conflict between a state and an armed group outside the state's own territory. These are mostly colonial conflicts.
- An interstate armed conflict is a conflict fought between two or more states. An intrastate armed conflict (also known as a civil conflict) is a conflict between a government and a non-state group that takes place largely within the territory of the state in question.
- An intrastate armed conflict becomes an internationalized intrastate armed conflict when the government, or an armed group opposing it, receives support, in the form of troops, from one or more foreign states.

What is Just war? Can any form of war be truly justified? When the ruler of a country arbitrarily kill his people, throw them into jail, annexes the territories of neighbouring countries, acts in ways inimical to public peace, human rights and the rule of law, there comes a time for international interventions. Such interventions begins with diplomacy. If such fails, force becomes a permissable means of exercising strength. Just wars could be relative. What some people consider just wars may be interpreted as bad wars. Such persons believe that no form of war could be justified. When the Rwanda massacre went on for a long time in 1994, the international community stood aloof. An estimated 800,000 Rwandans were killed in one of the world's most horrible genocides. By the time the world turned attention on Rwanda, it was already too late. Was the silence of the international community justified? Imagine how many lives could have been saved if the intervention came earlier! If the intervention had come earlier, it could have been an appropriate example of a Just war if it ended up up saving lives. Everyone has a right to life.

Former Swedish Prime Minister Ingvar Carlsson led the team that assessed the Rwandan genocide. His team included Han Sung-Joo the former South Korean Foreign Minister and Maj. Gen. Rufus Modupe Kupolati of Nigeria. Carlsson later summed up their findings by saying that *"Our conclusion is there is one overriding failure which explains why the UN could not stop or prevent the genocide, and that is a lack of resources and a lack of will - a*

---

[9] James A. Lucas, US Has Killed More Than 20 Million People in 37 "Victim Nations" Since World War II Global Research. November 09, 2017. https://www.globalresearch.ca/us-has-killed-more-than-20-million-people-in-37-victim-nations-since-world-war-ii/5 Retrieved 10 December 2017.
[10] English Oxford Dictionary, https://en.oxforddictionaries.com/definition/war Retrieved 10 December 2017.
[11] Max Roser (2016) – 'War and Peace'. *Published online at OurWorldInData.org.* https://ourworldindata.org/war-and-peace/ Retrieved 10 December 2017.

lack of will to take on the commitment necessary to prevent the genocide,"[12] When such delays occur, some persons that run the affairs of the United Nations should be held accountable. Even if a country is not a member of the UN, any infringement against the lives of others must not be ignored. Rwanda became a member of the United Nations on 18 September 1962. Article 3 of The Universal Declaration of Human Rights of the United Nations clearly states that *everyone has the right to life, liberty and security of person.*The UN report that assessed the genocide in Rwanda clearly *faulted the United Nations in several key areas leading up to that date, including its failure to act on a now-famous cable sent by the force commander, Canadian Lt. Gen. Romeo Dallaire on Jan. 11, 1994 warning of the risk of genocide. The cable was received by Annan and wasn't shared with the Security Council and didn't receive the follow-up such an important piece of evidence deserved, the report said. In addition, the United Nations and Security Council virtually ignored a groundbreaking assessment by the UN human rights investigator for Rwanda who raised the possibility in August 1993 that a genocide might occur.*[13]

It was after the genocide that Kofi Annan the then Secretary General of the United Nations expressed „deep remorse" for the delay of the United Nations in acting timeously in the Rwandan crises.

Some wars are fought for political reasons. The political ideology behind such wars could determine whether they are justified or not. The processes involved in such wars are also determinants. When innocent persons are killed in the process of embarking on a seemingly justified war, the essence of such justifications become questionable. Can a war be completely fought without the death of innocent persons?

When Nigeria embarked on the civil war of 1967 against the Biafran uprising, it was focused on the need to preserve the sovereignty of the country. One of the cardinal goals of every government is to ensure the unity and security of the country. The fundamental cause of the Nigerian civil war was that the country was hitherto, divided along ethnic lines through the colonialization of Britain. This became an internal divisive line among Nigerians. Any harm, perceived or real, done against a member of an ethnic group by a member of another ethnic group was easily seen as an ethnic affront with an aim to marginalize and oppress. So, when a coup headed by Major Kaduna Nzeogu occured in January 1966 and masterminded mainly by soldiers from the eastern part of the country, Nigeria's Prime Minister Sir Abubakar Tafawa Balewa, Northern premier Sir Ahmadu Bello and other notable persons of northern extraction were killed.

In July of that same year, military officers from the northern part of the country staged a counter-coup and installed General Yakubu Gowon a Muslim officer from central Nigeria as as the head of State. It was this counter coup that increased ethnic tensions among Nigerians. Int hat year, an estimated 30,000 Igbo were killed in the north. This was quickly followed by reprisal attacks in the east which witnessed the massacre of many northers who resided there.

---

[12] Nicole Winfield, <u>UN Failed Rwanda,</u> *Associated Press/ Nando Media* ,
https://www.globalpolicy.org/component/content/article/201/39240.html December 16, 1999. Retrieved 11 November 2017
[13] ibid.

Meanwhile, there has been ongoing grudges that the nation's wealth came from the Southern part of the country due to its rich oil deposits. This awareness instigated the southerners who felt that the northerners were receiving more than a fair share. The aftermath of these developments led to the declaration of the Republic of Biafra on 30 May 1967 led by Major Odumegwu Ojukwu. The Nigerian government forcefully stepped int o maintain the territorial integrity of the country by releasing her arsenals to quel the uprising. The response by the international community further increased the civil war. There was no international concesus on how to restore peace. While some countries supported the secession, others did not. Those that supported it it equally supplied equipments and other machineries of state to increase the tension. Once again, the United Nations as an umbrelly body could not speak with one voice. Unilateral actions were taken by its member states the exacerbate the tension. The so-called Republic of Biafran was formally recognised by countries like Ivory Coast, Tanzania, Haiti, Gabon, and Zambia. Among others, surreptitious supports were given by Israel, Norway, Rhodesia, Spain, South Africa, France, Portugal, and the Vatican City. It is note worthy that when the war ended, a new unarmed uprising occured mainly between 2016- 2017 led by one Nnamdi Kanu. He hinged most of his unofficial support on Israel.

When the war ended in 1970, it was estimated that over three million Biafrans died in the cause of the civil war. In such a war, it was a *Just War* in the interpretation of the Nigerian government while it was an unjustified War by the interpretation of the Biafrans who felt that they have a legal right to secede.

Various theories supports the justification of wars as a last resort. This is based on the underlying notion of using a certain and limited evil to fight a bigger evil.

Just War theory (Latin: *jus bellum iustum*) is a doctrine, also referred to as a tradition, of military ethics studied by military leaders, theologians, ethicists and policy makers. The purpose of the doctrine is to ensure war is morally justifiable through a series of criteria, all of which must be met for a war to be considered just. The criteria are split into two groups: "right to go to war" (*jus ad bellum*) and "right conduct in war" (*jus in bello*). The first concerns the morality of going to war, and the second the moral conduct within war[14]

Though there are various theories on Just Wars, I wish to hinge this research on two of such thoughts. This will be based on the theories of the *Salamanca School* of thought and that of *Saint Thomas Aquinas*. The aim of relying on these two theories is because they define Just Wars on the platform of moral, and theological points of view with a common denominator which is based on the respect for the preservation of life. This is especially so because they do not support wars based on the doctrine of expansion, glory, plundering or the forceful convertion of persons to certain religious belief.

The Salamanca School of thought reasoned that war should be a last resort, and only then, when necessary to prevent an even greater evil. Diplomatic resolution is always preferable, even for the more powerful party, before a war is started. Examples of "just war" are:

- In self-defense, as long as there is a reasonable possibility of success.
- Preventive war against a tyrant who is about to attack.
- War to punish a guilty enemy.

---

[14] Guthrie, Charles; Quinlan, Michael (26 Sep 2007). "III: The Structure of the Tradition". *Just War: The Just War Tradition: Ethics in Modern Warfare*. United Kingdom: Bloomsbury Publishing PLC. pp. 11–15.

A war is not legitimate or illegitimate simply based on its original motivation: it must comply with a series of additional requirements:

- It is necessary that the response be commensurate with the evil; use of more violence than is strictly necessary would constitute an unjust war.
- Governing authorities *declare* war, but their decision is not sufficient cause to begin a war. If the *people* oppose a war, then it is illegitimate. The people have a right to depose a government that is waging, or is about to wage, an unjust war.
- Once war has begun, there remain moral limits to action. For example, one may not attack innocents or kill hostages.
- It is obligatory to take advantage of all options for dialogue and negotiations before undertaking a war; war is only legitimate as a last resort.[15]

Saint Thomas Aquinas

Thomas Aquinas (1225–1274) conditions for Just Wars are as follows:

- First, just war must be waged by a properly instituted authority such as the state. (Proper Authority is first: represents the common good: which is peace for the sake of man's true end—God.)
- Second, war must occur for a good and just purpose rather than for self-gain (for example, "in the nation's interest" is not just) or as an exercise of power (just cause: for the sake of restoring some good that has been denied. i.e. lost territory, lost goods, punishment for an evil perpetrated by a government, army, or even the civilian populace).
- Third, peace must be a central motive even in the midst of violence. (right intention: an authority must fight for the just reasons it has expressly claimed for declaring war in the first place. Soldiers must also fight for this intention).[16]

The thrust underlining wars as 'just' lies in the postulation that *war, while terrible, is not always the worst option. Important responsibilities, undesirable outcomes, or preventable atrocities may justify war*[17]

The notion of Just War is as old as man. Research by Rory has shown that *"demonstrating that just war thought developed beyond the boundaries of Europe and existed many centuries earlier than the advent of Christianity or even the emergence of Greco-Roman doctrine.*[18]

Peace as a concept is vague and relative. Galtung (1967) defines the concept of „peace as a synonym for stability or equilibrium. This conception of peace also refers to internal states of a human being, the person who is at peace with himself. It also covers the "law and order"

---

[15] Thy, G, (2012, April 11). The Just War of Thomas Aquinas and Pacificm Arguments. *Theoplatz.* http://theosplatz.scenewash.org/2012/04/11/the-good-war-versus-pacifism/

[16] James T. Johnson, Just War, Encyclopædia Britannica, June 15, 2017 https://www.britannica.com/topic/just-war December 24, 2017

[17] Guthrie, Charles; Quinlan, Michael (26 Sep 2007). "III: The Structure of the Tradition". Just War: The Just War Tradition: Ethics in Modern Warfare. United Kingdom: Bloomsbury Publishing PLC. pp. 11–15.

[18]Cox, Rory (2017). „Expanding the History of the Just War: The Ethics of War in Ancient Egypt". *International Studies Quarterly.* 61(2): 371

concept, in other words the idea of a predictable social order even if this order is brought about by means of force and the threat of force."[19]

Galtung goes further to highlight the elements of Peace as comprising: *1.Presence of cooperation 2. Freedom from fear 3. Freedom from want 4. Economic growth and development 5. Absence of exploitation 6. Equality 7. Justice 8. Freedom of action 9. Pluralism 10. Dynamism*[20]

Could any form of peace be referred to as Bad Peace? After the victory of war, what next? Bad Peace is a situation that occurs when, after intervening in a conflict situation, peace efforts are not established and sustained. Any attempt to fight a war must by simultaneously juxtaposed with strategies to win the peace. Bad Peace is the situation that occured after the overthrow and killing of Muammar Gaddafi of Libya and the death of Sadam Hussain in Iraq. Bad Peace could also be described albeit by the renewed Biafran uprising of Nigeria about 50 years after the Nigerian civil Wars. Those same factors of proclaimed marginalization were the same reasons put forth by the Biafran agitators. Whether their position is correct, depends on the assessment by the efforts of the Nigerian government to fully integrate the Biafrans after the civil wars. However, it has been convincingly argued and evidenced by the fact that the Igbo tribe of Nigeria have been an integral part of governance at the local, State and Federal levels before and after the civil war. This argument was a common denominator that weakened and defeated the renewed quest for secesion decades after.

In the case of Libya, after the 2011 overthrow of Gaddafi with the support of Western powers, the coalition of militias have been fighting with the government; ISIS continue to terrorize and ravage oil installations, many have fled the countries as refugees, migrants attempting to cross through Libya to Europe have been killed and sold as slaves, militias and government forces have been locked in continuing battles. The expected peace has, ironically, led to a renewed conflict with the Western powers apparently confused about how to restore and sustain the needed peace, stability and development, which the violent overthrow of Gaddafi promised. *It is a war that has left 5,000 dead, the economy in ruins, half a million homeless and the dreams of 2011 shattered.*[21]

In Iraq, President Saddam Hussain was toppled by a US-led invasion in 2003; hanged around his neck and killed on 30 December 2006. What was acclaimed as a success of the Arab spring uprising, was envisioned to usher in a democratic, peaceful and more developed society. Sadly, bad peace evolved when the level of efforts applied to win and sustain the peace was not commensurate with the effort invested to overthrow Hussain. The Iraqis continue to live in terror, young persons are anxious to emigrate, the air is full with the thick fear of death; people are killed and dumped, sectarian warfare are on the increase superintended by the Sunni and Shia death squad; the continuing onslaught by al-Qaeda is

[19] Galtung, J. (1967). *Theory of Peace, A Synthetic Approach to Peace Thinking.* International Peace Research Institute,Oslo. p. 12
[20] ibid. p.14
[21] Chris Stephen, (16 February 2016) „Five years after Gaddafi, Libya thorn by civil war and battles with ISIS". *The Guardian.* https://www.theguardian.com/world/2016/feb/16/libya-gaddafi-arab-spring-civil-war-islamic-state. Retrieved 11 December 2017

unabated and the country's Sunni minority continue to demonstrate against their marginalization by the Shia-dominated government. These and a poorly equipped military and para-military force has left the contry worse off. Youths are very anxious to leave the country as *„ al-Qaeda has mounted repeated strikes across the country, with an average of 68 car bombs a month…"* [22]

The various conflict resolution strategies that were applied by Nigeria on peacekeeping, peace building and peace enforcement are worth mentioning. Between 1960 and 2017, budget for defence has increased with the challenges of the time.

As a way of enforcing peace in troubled Liberia, the Nigerian government under President Olusegun Obasanjo granted political asylum to Liberia's former President Charles Taylor in Nigeria as a way of taking him away from Liberia so that the peace process will progress unhindered. Taylor arrived Nigeria on 11 August 2003. Obasanjo granted this asylum for humanitarian and strategic reasons because it was the period when Liberian rebels had seized the ports and prevented humanitarian aids from reaching starving Liberians. It was after Taylor left for Nigeria that Liberian rebels surrendered the ports to Nigerian soldiers on August 14, 2003,[23] thereby permitting the entrance of humanitarian aids and paving the way for further meaningful reconcilliations.

It is also on record that another exiled warlord Yormie "Prince" Johnson, who was videotaped when he slayed former Liberian President Samuel Doe escaped to Lagos Nigeria as a way of dousing the tension in Liberia. Roosevelt Johnson, another former Liberian warlord and a rival of Charles Taylor also escaped to the Nigerian city of Jos at the height of tensions. They always saw Nigeria as a safe haven. However, granting asylum to Charles Taylor was followed by harsh criticisms and legal fire works as it challenged the impunity of granting asylum to war criminals.

Monthly security votes are given to the Federal and 36 States of Nigeria as a way of assisting them in securing various areas of the country and ensuring peace. However, these votes have been criticized as unconstitutional as it only duplicates the work of other security agencies,

The government ensures that the Internally Displaced Persons who fled the continuing attack by Boko Haram are given adequate care. Therefore, when Babachir Lawal. M. Lawal the Secretary to the Federal Government awarded corrupt contracts to himself with funds which ought to have improved the standard of life at the IDP camp, he was removed from office in October 2017.

---

[22] Collins Freeman, (12 December 2013), „Iraq still bleeding ten years after Saddam Hussain's capture". *The Telegraph. http://www.telegraph.co.uk/news/worldnews/middleeast/iraq/10514145/Iraq-is-still-bleeding-10-years-after-Saddam-Husseins-capture. Retrievved 15 December 2017*
[23] Shadare, W and Akpan, A. (2003, August 5), "Liberian Rebels Surrender Port to Nigerian Soldiers", *The Guardian Newspaper.*

10

The conflict between Nigeria and Cameroon over the ownership of the Bakassi peninsula was brewing into a war. Attacks and casualties were already reported. When the case was finally adjudicated by the International Court of Justice in favour of Cameroon, Nigeria under the government of President Olusegun Obasanjo ceded the disputed area to Cameroon in August 2008 despite the fact that it is an oil-rich region. Such efforts at peace enforcement endeared Nigeria to the international community.

The renewed agitation for the secession of Biafra from Nigeria worsened in 2017. The agitation led by Nnamdi Kanu led to the loss of lives and properties with various threats issued against the northerners who lived in the east and against easterners who lived in the north. A boycott order to future elections were issued by Kanu and the tension was gathering momentum. The government of Buhari secured a court order and declared all Biafran bodies as terrorist organizations. Kanu quickly disappeared and abruptly ended the prolonged agitation. What would have resulted into crises in the governorship election of November 2017 was quickly brought to an end. Meanwhile, various ammunitions were seized at the ports as they attempted to be smuggled into Nigeria from Turkey.[24]

At the height of the militancy in the Niger Delta region, many oil installations were vandalized, several persons were killed and others kidnapped for ransom. This created huge financial loss and insecurity in the Niger Delta. In order to enforce peace, the government of Nigeria granted amnesty to the agitators on the 6 of August 2009 during the government of President Umaru Yar'Adua. The militants were asked to surrender their arms for cash and they were put on monthly salaries in order to quell the agitations.[25] Though pockets of militancy resumed in 2016 because of the insatiability of the militants and reported political masterminding by politicians who desired to arm-twist the government, it was reported that oil pipeline vandalism from January to October 2016 caused Nigeria a loss of about t $7 billion[26]

In the international front, good peace was ensured when Nigeria led other West African countries to apply the instruments of conflict resolution to negotiate with the ousted President Yahya Jammeh to relinquish power to the elected President Adama Barrow who defeated him in the December election of 2016. This peace effort was made easy because the majority of Gambians supported external intervention. The West African force of 7,000 stayed in Gambia for six months after the installation of Barrow in order to sustain the peace from sliding into bad peace. This was especially so because there was palpable fear that loyalists to Jammeh and his Jola minority group could be targets of attack or supporters of violence.

[24] Usma, E; et al. (2017, 12 September) „Another 1100 Pump Action rifles seized in Lagos". *Vanguard Newspaper* https://www.vanguardngr.com/2017/09/another-1100-pump-action-rifles-seized-lagos *Retrieved 11 November 2017*
[25] Rice, X, (2009, August 6). „Nigeria begins amnesty for Niger Delta militants" *The Guardian*
[26] Agency report, (2016, October 28). „Nigeria loses N2.1 trillion to Niger Delta militants, vandals in 2016" *Premium Times.* https://www.premiumtimesng.com/news/headlines/213948-nigeria-loses-n2-1-trillion-niger-delta-militants-vandals-2016

The continuing Boko Haram uprising is currently a challenge in Nigeria though the government has offered a leeway for the militants to surrender. The fight against this sect suffered a major set back in 2015 when the £1.4bn set aside to fight the militants were diverted to campaign for the Presidential election of former President Jonathan Goodluck which he lost. The government of President Muhammadu Buhari has been forcing those involved to return the loot.[27]

Nigeria did not manage the conflict in the Ijaw village of Odi in Bayelsa State of Nigeria according to the rule of law. While the government of Obasanjo supported a return to normalcy in Liberia, on November 5, 1999 a hundred persons were massacred by the Nigerian soldiers deployed by Obasanjo's administration in Odi as they demonstrated on their rights to their oil resources. Though it was alleged that the villagers killed some police officers earlier, the reprisal attack on innocent villagers was not a commensurate legal action. The villagers went to court to seek redress. „*In February 2013, the Federal High Court ordered the Federal Government to pay N37.6 billion compensation to the people of Odi. In his judgment, Justice Lambi Akanbi condemned the government for a "brazen violation of the fundamental human rights of the victims to movement, life and to own property and live peacefully in their ancestral home.*"[28]

Indeed, a bad peace is worse than war![29]

---

[27] Agencies in Abuja. (2015, December 14). „Former Nigerian security official denies embezzling £1.4bn of arms money" *The Guardian*, https://www.theguardian.com/world/2015/dec/14/nigerian-security-money-goodluck-jonathan-boko-haram Retrieved 11 November 2017

[28] Ibekwe, N, (2013, February 20). Odi Massacre: Court orders Nigerian Government to pay N37bn damages to residents, *Premium Times*. https://www.premiumtimesng.com/news/121196-odi-massacre-court-orders-nigerian-government-to-pay-n37bn-damages-to-residents.

[29] Tacitus quotes, https://www.goodreads.com/quotes/543400-a-bad-peace-is-worse-than-war, n.d

Bibliography

Adeniyi. A, Peacekeeping Contributor Profile: Nigeria,
http://www.providingforpeacekeeping.org/2015/04/24/peacekeeping-contributor-profile-nigeria

Agencies in Abuja. (2015, December 14). „Former Nigerian security official denies embezzling
£1.4bn of arms money" *The Guardian*, https://www.theguardian.com/world/2015/dec/14/nigerian-security-money-goodluck-jonathan-boko-haram

Agency report, (2016, October 28). „Nigeria loses N2.1 trillion to Niger Delta militants, vandals in 2016"

Premium Times. https://www.premiumtimesng.com/news/headlines/213948-nigeria-loses-n2-1-trillion-niger-delta-militants-vandals-2016

Chris Stephen, (16 February 2016) „Five years after Gaddafi, Libya thorn by civil war and battles with ISIS". *The Guardian*. https://www.theguardian.com/world/2016/feb/16/libya-gaddafi-arab-spring-civil-war-islamic-state

Cox, Rory (2017). „Expanding the History of the Just War: The Ethics of War in Ancient Egypt".
International Studies Quarterly. 61(2): 371

English Oxford Dictionary, https://en.oxforddictionaries.com/definition/war

*Guthrie, Charles; Quinlan, Michael (26 Sep 2007). "III: The Structure of the Tradition". Just War:
The Just War Tradition: Ethics in Modern Warfare. United Kingdom: Bloomsbury Publishing PLC.
pp. 11–15.*

Galtung, J. (1967). *Theory of Peace, A Synthetic Approach to Peace Thinking*. International Peace
Research Institute,Oslo. p. 12

James T. Johnson, Just War, Encyclopædia Britannica, June 15, 2017
https://www.britannica.com/topic/just-war

James A. Lucas, US Has Killed More Than 20 Million People in 37 "Victim Nations" Since World
War II Global Research, November 09, 2017. https://www.globalresearch.ca/us-has-killed-more-than-20-million-people-in-37-victim-nations-since-world-war-ii/5

Ibekwe, N, (2013, February 20). Odi Massacre: Court orders Nigerian Government to pay N37bn
damages to residents, *Premium Times*. https://www.premiumtimesng.com/news/121196-odi-massacre-court-orders-nigerian-government-to-pay-n37bn-damages-to-residents.

King, B. (2005, April 22). *Daily Reckoning*, Benjamin Franklin, Diplomat: There Never Was a Good
War or a Bad Peace: Ben Franklin. https://dailyreckoning.com/benjamin-franklin-diplomat-there-never-was-a-good-war-or-a-bad-peace-ben-franklin/

Max Roser (2016) – 'War and Peace'. *Published online at OurWorldInData.org.*
https://ourworldindata.org/war-and-peace/

Nicole Winfield, UN Failed Rwanda, *Associated Press/ Nando Media* ,
https://www.globalpolicy.org/component/content/article/201/39240.html

Nigeria Police Force, http://www.npf.gov.ng/peace_keeping.php Retrieved 10 November 2017

Rice, X, (2009, August 6). „Nigeria begins amnesty for Niger Delta militants" *The Guardian*

Tacitus quotes, https://www.goodreads.com/quotes/543400-a-bad-peace-is-worse-than-war, n.d

Thy, G, (2012, April 11). The Just War of Thomas Aquinas and Pacificm Arguments. *Theoplatz.* http://theosplatz.scenewash.org/2012/04/11/the-good-war-versus-pacifism/

Usma, E; et al. (2017, 12 September) „Another 1100 Pump Action rifles seized in Lagos". *Vanguard Newspaper https://www.vanguardngr.com/2017/09/another-1100-pump-action-rifles-seized-lagos Retrieved 11 November 2017*

United Nations. http://www.un.org/en/history-united-nations/index.html Rerieved 11 November 2017

United Nations Peacekeeping. Principles of peacekeeping http://peacekeeping.un.org/en/principles-of-peacekeeping Retrieved 10 November 2017

United Nations Peacekeeping. Mandate and the legal basis for peacekeeping http://peacekeeping.un.org/en/mandates-and-legal-basis-peacekeeping. Retrieved 10 November 2017

United Nations. http://www.un.org/en/history-united-nations/index.html Rerieved 11 November 2017

United Nations Peacekeeping. Principles of peacekeeping http://peacekeeping.un.org/en/principles-of-peacekeeping Retrieved 10 November 2017

United Nations Peacekeeping. Mandate and the legal basis for peacekeeping http://peacekeeping.un.org/en/mandates-and-legal-basis-peacekeeping. Retrieved 10 November 2017

,